United States Government Accountability Office

# GAO

Report to the Chairman, Subcommittee on Near Eastern and South and Central Asian Affairs, Committee on Foreign Relations, U.S. Senate

May 2012

# COMBATING TERRORISM

I0426235

# State Should Enhance Its Performance Measures for Assessing Efforts in Pakistan to Counter Improvised Explosive Devices

**GAO**

Accountability * Integrity * Reliability

**GAO**
Accountability * Integrity * Reliability

# Highlights

Highlights of GAO-12-614, a report to the Chairman, Subcommittee on Near Eastern and South and Central Asian Affairs, Committee on Foreign Relations, U.S. Senate

# COMBATING TERRORISM

## State Should Enhance Its Performance Measures for Assessing Efforts in Pakistan to Counter Improvised Explosive Devices

## Why GAO Did This Study

Improvised explosive devices have been a significant cause of fatalities among U.S. troops in Afghanistan. About 80 percent of the IEDs contain homemade explosives, primarily calcium ammonium nitrate (CAN) fertilizer smuggled from Pakistan. U.S. officials recognize the threat posed by the smuggling of CAN and other IED precursors from Pakistan into Afghanistan, and State and other agencies are assisting Pakistan's government to counter this threat. This report (1) describes the status of U.S. efforts to assist Pakistan in countering IEDs and (2) reviews State's tracking of U.S. assisted efforts in Pakistan to counter IEDs. To address these objectives, GAO reviewed agency strategy and programmatic documents, including State's fiscal year 2013 MSRP for Pakistan. GAO also met with U.S. officials in Washington, D.C., Arlington, Virginia, and Tampa, Florida; and met with U.S. and Pakistani officials in Islamabad, Pakistan.

## What GAO Recommends

To improve State's ability to track progress of efforts in Pakistan to counter IEDs, GAO recommends that the Secretary of State direct the U.S. Mission in Pakistan to enhance its counter-IED performance measures to cover the full range of U.S. assisted efforts. State concurred and committed to look for ways to broaden the scope of existing metrics in order to better reflect and evaluate interagency participation in counter-IED efforts.

View GAO-12-614. View related video clip. For more information, contact Charles Michael Johnson, Jr. at (202) 512-7331 or johnsoncm@gao.gov.

## What GAO Found

Multiple U.S. agencies and international partners are engaged in efforts to assist Pakistan in countering improvised explosive devices (IEDs) but face a variety of ongoing challenges. The agencies providing counter-IED assistance to Pakistan are primarily the Departments of State (State), Defense (DOD), Homeland Security (DHS), and Justice (DOJ). The following table identifies the types of assistance these U.S. agencies have provided and the corresponding objectives of Pakistan's National Counter-IED Strategy. According to U.S. officials, U.S. agencies have encountered ongoing challenges to their efforts to assist Pakistan, such as delays in obtaining visas and in the delivery of equipment. U.S. officials have also identified broader challenges to Pakistan's ability to counter IEDs, including the extreme difficulty of interdicting smugglers along its porous border with Afghanistan. In addition, though Pakistan developed a National Counter-IED Strategy in June 2011, it has yet to finalize an implementation plan for carrying out the strategy.

**Types of U.S. Assistance to Pakistan to Counter IEDs**

| U.S. assistance efforts | Objectives of Pakistan counter-IED strategy |
|---|---|
| Counter-IED training and/or equipment | Engage the international community for equipment, training, and capacity building in the area of counter-IEDs |
| Counter-IED public awareness campaign | Launch a vigorous counter-IED public awareness campaign |
| Training of border officials | Control cross-border movement of IEDs, accessories, smuggling of ammonium nitrate and other precursors |
| Legal assistance for laws and regulations to counter IEDs and IED precursors | Modify the existing legislative framework by strengthening legislation on terrorism and explosives |

Source: GAO analysis based on documents and interviews.

The U.S. fiscal year 2013 Mission Strategic and Resource Plan (MSRP) for Pakistan includes a new performance indicator to track some of Pakistan's efforts to counter IEDs, but the indicator and targets used to measure progress do not cover the full range of U.S. assisted efforts. The performance indicator focuses on cross-border activities, specifically on Pakistan's efforts to prevent illicit commerce in sensitive materials, including chemical precursors used to manufacture IEDs in Afghanistan. As such, progress of U.S. counter-IED assistance efforts not specifically linked to cross-border smuggling are not covered, such as counter-IED training and/or equipment, a counter-IED public awareness campaign, and legal assistance for laws and regulations to counter-IEDs and IED precursors. Consequently, effects of key U.S. assisted counter-IED efforts are not tracked under the existing performance indicator and related targets. The absence of comprehensive performance measures that reflect the broad range of U.S. assisted counter-IED efforts limits State's ability to track overall progress in Pakistan to counter IEDs and to determine the extent to which these counter-IED efforts are helping to achieve the U.S. goals.

# Contents

## Abbreviations

| | |
|---|---|
| CAN | calcium ammonium nitrate |
| CENTCOM | Central Command |
| DHS | Department of Homeland Security |
| DOD | Department of Defense |
| DOJ | Department of Justice |
| IED | improvised explosive device |
| JIEDDO | Joint Improvised Explosive Device Defeat Organization |
| MSRP | Mission Strategic and Resource Plan |
| ODRP | Office of the Defense Representative, Pakistan |
| SOCOM | Special Operations Command |
| State | Department of State |

## View GAO-12-614 Component

Video showing the border region and activity at the primary border crossings.

May 15, 2012

The Honorable Robert P. Casey, Jr.
Chairman
Subcommittee on Near Eastern and South
    and Central Asian Affairs
Committee on Foreign Relations
United States Senate

Dear Mr. Chairman:

Improvised explosive devices (IEDs) have been a significant cause of fatalities among U.S. troops in Afghanistan. About 80 percent of the IEDs contain homemade explosives, primarily calcium ammonium nitrate (CAN) fertilizer smuggled from Pakistan. U.S. officials recognize the threat posed by the smuggling of CAN and other IED precursors from Pakistan into Afghanistan, and the Department of State (State) and other agencies are assisting Pakistan's government to counter this threat. In addition, with the adoption in 2011 of its National Counter-IED Strategy, Pakistan recognized the importance of addressing the IED threat, both for its own security and stability goals, as well as for counterterrorism efforts in the region. Various insurgent groups in Pakistan regularly use IEDs, which have killed thousands of Pakistani civilians and security force members.

In your November 2010 hearing on this issue, officials from State and the Departments of Defense (DOD) and Homeland Security (DHS) testified about the flow of CAN from Pakistan into Afghanistan as well as the need for Pakistan to step up its efforts to address the IED threat. Since then, senior U.S. officials have continued to raise this issue with Pakistani counterparts. Recognizing the importance of this issue, you asked us to report on U.S. agencies' efforts to provide counter-IED assistance to Pakistan, including development of Pakistan's National Counter-IED Strategy and the follow-on plan to implement that strategy. In this report, we (1) describe the status of U.S. efforts to assist Pakistan in countering IEDs and (2) review State's tracking of U.S. assisted efforts in Pakistan to counter IEDs.

To describe the status of U.S. efforts to assist Pakistan in countering IEDs, we reviewed documentation from multiple U.S. agencies to inventory and describe their relevant activities. In addition, we reviewed the Pakistan National Counter-IED Strategy and draft National

Implementation Plan to gain knowledge of the areas that Pakistan has focused on in seeking assistance from the international community. We analyzed U.S. agencies' funding and program information on specific projects that assist Pakistan in these efforts and followed up with interviews with knowledgeable U.S. officials and international partners, including officials from State, DHS, and the Department Justice (DOJ) in Washington, D.C., and from DOD in Arlington, Virginia, and Tampa, Florida. We also interviewed representatives of all these agencies and the U.S. Department of Agriculture at the U.S. Embassy in Pakistan. In addition, while conducting fieldwork in Pakistan, we interviewed Pakistani customs officials to obtain their perspective on counter-IED efforts and challenges, and we met with representatives of the Pakistan Trade Project and the Pakistan National Fertilizer Development Center. Finally, we also interviewed officials from the United Nations Office on Drugs and Crime, the British High Commission, and the International Security Assistance Force International Coordination Element–Pakistan.

To review State's tracking of U.S. assisted efforts in Pakistan to counter IEDs, we reviewed State's fiscal year 2013 Mission Strategic and Resource Plan (MSRP) for the U.S. Mission in Pakistan. Specifically, we reviewed goals, performance indicators, and targets for counterterrorism and counterinsurgency; regional security, stability, and nonproliferation; law enforcement reform and rule of law; and public diplomacy and strategic communications to identify the extent to which they covered counter-IED efforts. We also followed up with a State official at the U.S. Embassy in Pakistan with regard to how targets under the new counter-IED performance indicator in the MSRP track progress of counter-IED efforts.

We conducted this performance audit from October 2011 to May 2012 in accordance with generally accepted government auditing standards. Those standards require that we plan and perform the audit to obtain sufficient, appropriate evidence to provide a reasonable basis for our findings and conclusions based on our audit objectives. We believe that the evidence obtained provides a reasonable basis for our findings and conclusions based on our audit objectives.

## Background

Since 2001, Pakistan has been a U.S. ally in the fight against al Qaeda and a recipient of both civilian and military assistance. Key areas where both countries share common concerns include IEDs, which not only cause the majority of fatalities among U.S. troops in Afghanistan but have also caused thousands of fatalities in Pakistan. According to DOD, about

16,500 IEDs were detonated or discovered being used against U.S. forces in Afghanistan in 2011. About 80 percent of the IEDs used in Afghanistan have homemade explosives as the main charge, and more than 80 percent of these are derived from CAN fertilizer produced in Pakistan. The President of Afghanistan issued a decree outlawing CAN fertilizer in 2010.

According to DOD, CAN is produced in Pakistan at two factories, each generating between 463,000 and 496,000 tons[1] annually. DOD estimates that as little as 240 tons of CAN—representing less than one-tenth of 1 percent of the total annual production capacity of these two factories—is used to make IEDs in Afghanistan. According to officials from the National Fertilizer Development Center in Pakistan, less than 10 percent of the fertilizer used in Pakistan is CAN, but CAN is well suited for farmers in some areas. Figure 1 shows a bag of CAN, which is typically packaged in 110-pound bags. When processed and mixed with fuel oil, CAN fertilizer becomes a powerful homemade explosive.

---

[1] U.S. tons.

**Figure 1: Bag of CAN Fertilizer**

Source: DHS.

According to U.S. Department of Agriculture officials, Pakistan prohibits fertilizer producers from exporting CAN to Afghanistan or any other country. According to these officials, because there is a demand for CAN in Afghanistan for use as fertilizer and for the manufacture of IEDs, it is smuggled into Afghanistan, for example, on trucks hidden under other goods. U.S. officials said that Pakistan maintains two primary border crossings along the approximately 1,500-mile border with Afghanistan, and only a small percentage of the trucks crossing the border are inspected. U.S. officials also believe that CAN is smuggled into Afghanistan at multiple points along the porous border in the same way that other contraband, including consumer goods and narcotics, is trafficked across the border. See figure 2 for a map showing the Afghanistan-Pakistan border and the two primary border crossings. (See a video clip showing the border region and activity at the primary border crossings.)

**Figure 2: Map of Pakistan and Afghanistan Showing the Two Primary Border Crossings**

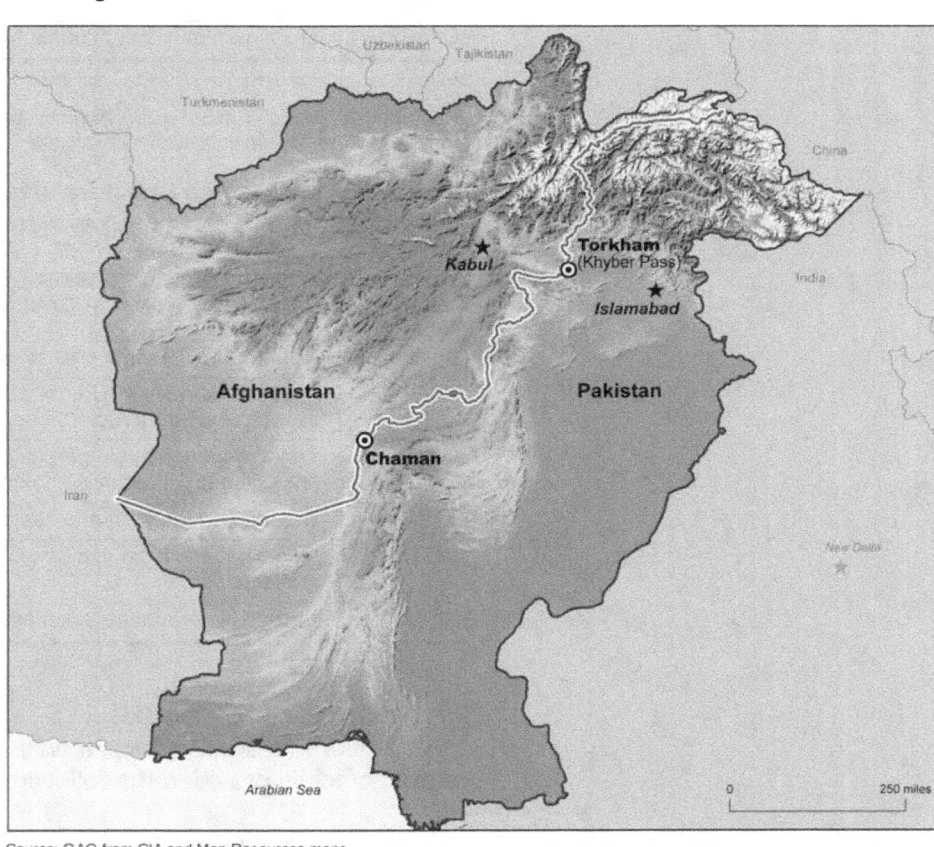

Source: GAO from CIA and Map Resources maps.

In response to the threat that IEDs pose to both security forces and civilians, the Government of Pakistan adopted a National Counter-IED Strategy in June 2011. The strategy identifies objectives and specific areas of effort to counter IEDs and prevent the smuggling of CAN and other precursors out of the country. Table 1 lists the objectives contained in Pakistan's counter-IED strategy.

**Table 1: Objectives of Pakistan's National Counter-IED Strategy**

| |
|---|
| Engage the international community for equipment, training, and capacity building in the area of counter-IEDs, (including the establishment of a National IED Exploitation Facility)[a] |
| Launch a vigorous counter-IED public awareness campaign |
| Control cross-border movement of IEDs, accessories, smuggling of ammonium nitrate and other precursors (including attacking the insurgents' network) |
| Modify the existing legislative framework by strengthening legislation on terrorism and explosives |
| Carry out effective interagency coordination (Pakistani government) |

Sources: GAO analysis of Government of Pakistan documents.

[a]The National IED Exploitation Facility would be an advanced laboratory able to exploit chemical, technical, biometric, and documentary evidence.

Multiple U.S. agencies assist Pakistan in countering IEDs. Table 2 summarizes the roles of the key agencies.

**Table 2: Key U.S. Agency Roles for Counter-IED Efforts**

| Agency | Role in counter-IED efforts in Pakistan |
|---|---|
| State | Advocacy through diplomatic channels with various Pakistani ministries; training and infrastructure support; public diplomacy |
| DOD | Training and equipping Pakistani forces to be able to interdict contraband (including IED precursors) along the Afghanistan-Pakistan border |
| DHS | Border management and customs investigation training |
| DOJ | Technical and legal expertise, forensic investigations, and criminal prosecutions |
| Agriculture | Technical assistance, such as providing alternative fertilizers to CAN |

Source: GAO analysis based on interviews with agency officials.

According to agency officials, U.S. agencies work through various organizations to share information in assisting Pakistan with counter-IED efforts; officials provided the following information on them:

- *U.S. Embassy-Pakistan Counter-IED Working Group* helps keeps counter-IED efforts a priority. Coordinated by State, participants also include DOD (Office of Defense Representative, Pakistan (ODRP), and Special Interagency Assistance Team); DOJ (Federal Bureau of Investigation and Drug Enforcement Administration); DHS; the Department of Agriculture; and the U.S. Agency for

International Development; as well as the British High Commission and the United Nations Office on Drugs and Crime.

- *Joint Improvised Explosive Device Defeat Organization (JIEDDO)*[2] leads DOD's counter-IED efforts by providing intelligence and expertise on IEDs. For example, JIEDDO hosted a conference on homemade explosives in Crystal City, Virginia, in fall 2011 that was attended by fertilizer producers and representatives from several agencies. JIEDDO conducted several studies and provided technical assistance to fertilizer producers on how they could identify the product to help inhibit smuggling.

- *Office of the Special Representative for Afghanistan and Pakistan* participates in regular discussions on counter-IED issues with Central Command (CENTCOM), Special Operations Command (SOCOM), JIEDDO, and the Counter-IED Working Group at the U.S. Embassy in Pakistan. In addition, officials from this office work with the Office of the Secretary of Defense for Policy to ensure that the highest levels in the U.S. and Pakistani governments remain focused on counter-IED issues, including efforts to disrupt the smuggling of CAN and other IED precursors from Pakistan to Afghanistan.

- *CENTCOM Interagency Action Group* works with other agencies to coordinate activities with its antiterrorism activities, including counter-IED efforts.

- *SOCOM Interagency Task Force* tracks trends that are collected by intelligence agencies, including the number of IED attacks, injuries, and deaths. In addition, the task force raises awareness of the issue of IEDs with multiple U.S. agencies to address the smuggling of CAN and other IED precursor materials.

## U. S. Agencies Face Ongoing Challenges Assisting Pakistan in Countering IEDs

Multiple U.S. agencies and international partners are engaged in efforts to assist Pakistan in countering IEDs but face various ongoing challenges. The U.S. agencies—primarily State, DHS, DOJ, and DOD—have provided counter-IED assistance to Pakistan, including counter-IED training and/or equipment, funding and development for a counter-IED public awareness campaign, training of border officials, and making legal advice available on drafting laws and regulations to counter IEDs.

---

[2]JIEDDO is an agency of DOD.

However, according to U.S. officials, these U.S. agencies have encountered ongoing challenges to their efforts to assist Pakistan, such as delays in obtaining visas and in the delivery of equipment. U.S. officials have also identified broader challenges to Pakistan's ability to counter IEDs, including the extreme difficulty of interdicting smugglers along its porous border with Afghanistan. In addition, though Pakistan developed a National Counter-IED Strategy in June 2011, it has yet to finalize an implementation plan for carrying out the strategy.

## Multiple Agencies and International Partners Are Assisting Pakistan to Counter IEDs

Multiple U.S. agencies and international partners are providing assistance to Pakistan to counter IEDs. Table 3 identifies the types of assistance U.S. agencies have provided and the objectives of Pakistan's National Counter-IED Strategy that these assistance efforts help address.

**Table 3: Types of U.S. Assistance to Pakistan to Counter IEDs**

| U.S. assistance efforts | U.S. agencies providing assistance | Objectives of Pakistan's National Counter-IED Strategy |
|---|---|---|
| Counter-IED training and/or equipment | State, DHS, DOJ, and DOD | Engage the international community for equipment, training, and capacity building in the area of counter-IEDs |
| Counter-IED public awareness campaign | State | Launch a vigorous counter-IED public awareness campaign |
| Training of border officials | State, DHS, and DOD | Control cross-border movement of IEDs, accessories, smuggling of ammonium nitrate and other precursors |
| Legal assistance for laws and regulations to counter IEDs and IED precursors | DOJ and DOD | Modify the existing legislative framework by strengthening legislation on terrorism and explosives |

Source: GAO analysis based on documents and interviews.

**Counter-IED training and/or equipment.** For example, DOD, through ODRP, is partnering with the United Kingdom to establish a counter-IED Center of Excellence at the Military College of Engineering in Risalpur, Pakistan. According to British officials, the Center would establish a "train the trainer" program to build the capacity of the Pakistan military and police forces to develop, gather, and use intelligence; attack networks; and search, dispose of, and study the forensics of IEDs. According to an ODRP official, the United Kingdom has already provided funding to establish the Center and provided the initial training portion of the Center's program. According to DOD, State has allocated $25 million in training and equipment for the Center's program. In addition ODRP purchased 110 IED jammers—devices that block the detonation of remote-controlled IEDs—for Pakistan, but the delivery of this equipment has been delayed. Other U.S. procured counter-IED equipment under review and still in U.S. storage includes kits for use by combined explosive exploitation cells, explosive ordnance disposal items, and portable trace explosive detectors. Additional counter-IED equipment procured by ODRP is still in production, such as counter-IED route clearance vehicles costing a total of about $63.9 million and additional remote controlled IED jammers costing about $12.1 million. Further, DOJ has also provided counter-IED training. For instance, DOJ's Drug Enforcement Administration (DEA) provided explosive ordnance disposal and IED identification training to a number of Pakistan's Anti-Narcotics Force Special Investigative Cell members in 2011. This training was provided by FBI's Legal Attaché office in Pakistan. DEA has provided investigative training and mentors for Pakistan's Anti-Narcotics Force Special Investigative Cell investigators, who have uncovered some linkages to IED networks and other terrorist activities.

**Counter-IED public awareness campaign.** In November 2011, State's Public Affairs Section of the U.S. Embassy in Pakistan launched a $1.3 million public awareness campaign using television, radio, and print media to communicate messages aimed at countering violent extremism and the use of IEDs in Pakistan. The campaign consisted of three phases: (1) define the IED problem, (2) create a forum to discuss the problem, and (3) empower citizens to detect and report threats to the local military and law enforcement authorities. According to State officials, the initial phase of the campaign focused on placing messages defining the IED problem on commercial stations, but Pakistan's Ministry of Information and Broadcasting has also aired some of them on state-run media. According to State officials, the campaign may be extended beyond its initial 6-month time frame, which was to end in May 2012, due to the positive response of the Pakistani public.

**Training of border officials.** Multiple U.S. agencies have provided training to Pakistani border officials. For instance, DHS conducts joint regional training and operational exercises for both Pakistani and Afghan border officials, including international border interdiction training and cross-border financial investigation training. According to a State official,

DHS also plays a lead role in Program Global Shield[3] to foster cross-border cooperation and initiate complementary border management and customs operations. In November 2011, DHS and State sponsored an International Visitors Leadership Program in the United States for Pakistani and Afghan border management and customs officials. According to ODRP officials, ODRP has provided training and equipment to Pakistani forces including Frontier Scouts active in the western border region, to enhance their capability to interdict contraband, including CAN and other IED precursor materials.

**Legal assistance for laws and regulations to counter-IEDs and IED precursors.** DOD and DOJ have made available legal assistance to Pakistan to advance its efforts to counter IEDs. ODRP's Strategic Interagency Assistance Team is prepared to provide legal advice in drafting laws and regulations with regard to the use, production, and transportation of IED precursor chemicals and other explosives, as well as in areas relating to the arrest and prosecution of persons engaged in the IED supply and production chain. According to DOJ officials, they are also available to provide additional legal assistance as needed.

## Agencies Face a Variety of Ongoing Challenges to Assisting Pakistan to Counter IEDs

U.S. agencies have encountered some challenges to providing assistance to Pakistan to counter IEDs, and events over the past 6 months have strained this important bilateral relationship. U.S. officials in Washington, D.C., and Pakistan identified four key difficulties that hamper the provision of training and equipment.

- *Obtaining visas for U.S. officials.* We have previously reported that U.S. officials face delays in obtaining visas to travel to Pakistan.[4]

---

[3]Program Global Shield is an international effort to counter the smuggling of chemical precursors that could be used to manufacture IEDs, including CAN. The World Customs Organization, the United Nations Office on Drugs and Crime, Interpol, and DHS jointly initiated this project in 2010 and established it as a program in June 2011 with funding of about $5.9 million that State provided through its Bureau of International Narcotics and Law Enforcement Affairs, according to the Bureau's Global Shield liaison officer. According to DHS, the main goals of Program Global Shield are (1) to identify and interdict falsely declared explosive precursor chemicals, (2) to initiate investigations of smuggled or illegally diverted IED materials, and (3) to uncover the smuggling and procurement networks that foster illicit trade.

[4]GAO, *Accountability for U.S. Equipment Provided to Pakistani Security Forces in the Western Frontier Needs to Be Improved,* GAO-11-156R (Washington, D.C.: Feb. 15, 2011).

During our January 2012 meetings at the U.S. Embassy, officials from several agencies told us that it is difficult to obtain visas for U.S. officials to travel to Pakistan, including trainers. One official stated that obtaining Pakistani visas for contractors providing services, including training, is persistently a challenge. According to officials, visa renewals sometimes take up to 6 weeks, which can force trainers to leave the country until they get their visa renewed. This has sometimes resulted in disruptions and cancelled training courses that has slowed the progress of U.S. efforts to initiate training programs and strengthen working relationships with Pakistani counterparts.

- *Vetting Pakistani officials to receive U.S. training.* U.S. law requires that U.S. agencies determine whether there is credible evidence of gross violations of human rights by security force units or individuals slated to receive security assistance.[5] According to U.S. officials, Pakistan must provide in advance the names of individuals who will be receiving U.S. training in order for them to be vetted. In addition U.S. officials stated that Pakistan has not always been timely in releasing the names of its officials who are to be the recipients of the training, which can create logistics and scheduling difficulties. For example, according to DHS officials, lack of sufficient time to complete the vetting process resulted in the cancellation of a Program Global Shield training session in October 2011.

- *Ensuring timely delivery of equipment.* Problems clearing customs and other issues have delayed the transfer of counter-IED equipment from the United States to Pakistani forces. For example, as of April 2012, of the 110 IED jammers that ODRP procured in 2009 for Pakistan at a cost of about $22.8 million, 55 Jammers were still in Karachi awaiting release from Pakistani customs, and the remaining 55 jammers were being kept in storage in the United States until the initial 55 were released.

- *Reaching agreement on the specifics of U.S. assistance projects.* Efforts by the United States to reach agreement with Pakistan on the specific terms of assistance projects can be challenging, as illustrated by the breakdown in efforts to establish an advanced IED exploitation

---

[5]See 22 U.S.C. 2378d regarding assistance furnished under the Foreign Assistance Act or the Arms Export Control Act. For programs funded by DOD appropriations, the provision is limited to training programs and is incorporated annually in the Department of Defense Appropriations Act. See, for example, Pub. L. No. 112-10, Div. A. sec. 8058.

facility. The United States and Pakistan planned to establish a facility capable of exploiting chemical, technical, biometric, and documentary evidence to enable Pakistan to disrupt insurgent networks. According to DOD officials, once it became clear that the United States and Pakistan could not reach agreement on joint use of the facility, DOD terminated its support for establishing this facility.

In addition to these challenges to U.S. efforts to assist Pakistan, U.S. officials identified several broader challenges to Pakistan's ability to counter IEDs in general and, more specifically, to suppress the smuggling of CAN and other IED precursors across its border with Afghanistan.

- *Finalizing Pakistan's National Counter-IED Implementation Plan.* While Pakistan's Directorate General for Civil Defense has developed a National Counter-IED Implementation Plan as outlined in the National Counter-IED Strategy, as of April 2012, the plan had not been approved due to concerns over resourcing and other issues. This plan would establish the various provincial, divisional, and district counter-IED cells that would monitor, analyze, and disseminate information on IEDs at the national, regional, and local levels. Pakistan's adoption of its implementation plan is needed to allow U.S. agencies to align their efforts with Pakistan's.

- *History of smuggling across the Pakistan-Afghanistan border.* The border between Pakistan and Afghanistan is approximately 1,500 miles long and much of the rugged mountainous terrain along the central and northern border is difficult to patrol. There is a history of smuggling goods in both directions at many points along this porous border. According to those involved with monitoring or interdicting this covert movement of goods, it is likely that CAN and other IED precursors are viewed as illicit commodities, like narcotics, to be smuggled for financial gain.

- *Small amount of CAN needed to make IEDs.* DOD officials noted that only a small amount of CAN is required to make powerful IEDs. According to DOD, a 110-pound bag of CAN yields about 82 pounds of bomb-ready explosive material. Packed in palm oil jugs, this small quantity has the capacity to destroy an armored vehicle or detonate 10 small blasts aimed at U.S. forces conducting foot patrols.

- *Substitutes for CAN available to make IEDs.* Even if the smuggling of CAN could be suppressed, insurgents could readily switch to another precursor chemical to make IEDs. According to DOD, other products available in Pakistan such as potassium chlorate, used in making matches, and urea, which is another commonly used fertilizer, can also be used to produce IEDs. At a JIEDDO conference on homemade explosives, a panel of experts agreed that insurgents could easily substitute these commodities to make IEDs if it becomes more difficult for them to access CAN.

- *IED precursors can be imported or smuggled into Afghanistan from other bordering countries.* While Pakistan is the principal source of CAN coming into Afghanistan, China and Iran are also reported to be suppliers of IED precursor chemicals. According to State officials, other substitutes for CAN, including urea and potassium chlorate, are exported by countries other than Pakistan.

## State's Strategic Document Includes Performance Measures for Some U.S. Assisted Counter-IED Efforts in Pakistan, but Other Key Areas Are Not Covered

The U.S. fiscal year 2013 MSRP for Pakistan included a new performance indicator to track some of Pakistan's efforts to counter IEDs, but the indicator and targets used to measure progress did not cover the full range of U.S. assisted efforts. According to State, each year every embassy develops its MSRP for the fiscal year two years out; this is done to facilitate long-term diplomatic and assistance planning.[6] The MSRP lays out the U.S. vision for the bilateral relationship and identifies and establishes broad goals and corresponding performance indicators with specific targets for monitoring progress. State reports that its Washington, D.C.-based bureaus draw on MSRPs to gauge the effectiveness of policies and programs in the field and to formulate requests for resources.

The MSRP for Pakistan included several goals, such as counterterrorism/counterinsurgency; regional security, stability, and nonproliferation; law enforcement reform and rule of law; and public diplomacy and strategic communications. Each of these goals included corresponding performance indicators and targets. In the MSRP for fiscal year 2013, State included—under its goal for regional security, stability, and nonproliferation—a new performance indicator and three targets to track some U.S. assisted Pakistani counter-IED efforts.

Specifically, the fiscal year 2013 MSRP included a performance indicator to monitor Pakistan's implementation of effective measures to prevent illicit commerce in sensitive materials, including chemical precursors used

---

[6]Thus, according to a State official, the fiscal year 2013 MSRP for Pakistan was finalized in 2011.

to make IEDs in Afghanistan. To measure progress toward this performance indicator, the fiscal year 2013 MSRP included three targets: (1) implementation of the Afghanistan-Pakistan Transit Trade Agreement for fiscal year 2011, (2) improved competency of Pakistani customs and border officials and improved monitoring at border stations for fiscal year 2012, and (3) Pakistan's implementation of a real-time truck-tracking system for fiscal year 2013. According to a State official at the U.S. Embassy in Pakistan, the 2013 MSRP's inclusion of a target for implementation of the Afghanistan-Pakistan Transit Trade Agreement had implications for countering IEDs because the agreement included measures aimed at reducing smuggling.

While the inclusion of a counter-IED performance indicator and targets to measure progress toward the indicator in the fiscal year 2013 MSRP is a positive step, it does not reflect the broad range of U.S. assisted counter-IED efforts in Pakistan. The existing performance indicator is focused on cross-border activities, specifically, Pakistan's efforts to prevent illicit commerce in sensitive materials, including precursors used to manufacture IEDs in Afghanistan; however, the indicator does not explicitly address other key counter-IED efforts in Pakistan. Progress of U.S. counter-IED assistance efforts not specifically linked to cross-border smuggling are not covered, such as counter-IED training and/or equipment, a counter-IED public awareness campaign, and legal assistance for laws and regulations to counter-IEDs and IED precursors. For example, while some of these efforts are included in the MSRP under other goals, they are not tracked to gauge progress toward counter-IED objectives.[7] Consequently, the effects of key U.S. assisted counter-IED efforts, including the development of the Counter-IED Center of Excellence at the Military College of Engineering in Risalpur, Pakistan, and the provision of IED jammers, are not tracked under the existing performance indicators and targets.

The absence of comprehensive performance measures reflecting the broad range of U.S. assisted counter-IED efforts limits State's ability to assess overall progress in Pakistan to counter IEDs and to determine the

---

[7]The fiscal year 2013 MSRP includes performance measures for a general public diplomacy campaign against violent extremism; however, targets did not include counter-IED efforts. In addition, the MSRP included a target on police training, counternarcotics, and prison reform that referenced counter-IED efforts, but the target is used to track Pakistan's progress on law enforcement reform.

extent to which these counter-IED efforts help achieve the U.S. goal of regional security, stability, and nonproliferation in Pakistan.

## Conclusions

Pakistan's ability to stem the flow of CAN and other IED precursors is a life and death issue for U.S. and coalition troops in Afghanistan. Despite a broad range of U.S. assisted efforts undertaken by Pakistan, IEDs made from CAN and other precursor chemicals smuggled in from Pakistan continue to remain a significant cause of fatalities among U.S. troops in Afghanistan. Multiple U.S. agencies and international partners are assisting Pakistan in countering IEDs, and Pakistan has developed its own National Counter-IED Strategy. However, U.S. efforts to assist Pakistan in implementing effective measures to prevent illicit commerce in IED precursors, including CAN, continue to face a spectrum of challenges. Some difficulties are narrower in scope, such as delays in obtaining and renewing visas for U.S. officials and trainers or reaching agreement on the specific terms for key projects. Other challenges are broader and more complex, such as the porous border between Pakistan and Afghanistan and the ready availability of IED precursors that can be smuggled across that border, of which only a small amount is needed to produce multiple IEDs. These challenges highlight how critically important it is that Pakistan finalize its National Counter-IED Implementation Plan to facilitate concrete actions necessary to achieve the objectives outlined in its National Counter-IED Strategy.

State has demonstrated the depth of the U.S. commitment to assist Pakistan in countering IEDs, as evidenced by the fiscal year 2013 MSRP for Pakistan, which included a new performance indicator and some targets to track the progress of some of Pakistan's counter-IED efforts. However, these performance metrics only partially capture the progress of counter-IED efforts in Pakistan. Enhancing performance measures to ensure that they provide a more comprehensive view of the progress and effect of U.S. assisted efforts could yield additional insights needed to refine the U.S. approach to assisting Pakistan in countering IEDs and to determine the extent to which these efforts further U.S. goals.

## Recommendation for Executive Action

To improve State's ability to track progress of efforts in Pakistan to counter IEDs, we recommend that the Secretary of State direct the U.S. Mission in Pakistan to enhance its counter-IED performance measures to cover the full range of U.S. assisted efforts.

## Agency Comments

We provided a draft of this report to State, DHS, DOD, and DOJ. State and DHS provided written comments, which are reproduced in appendixes II and III, respectively. State concurred with our recommendation and noted that comprehensive metrics would better enable evaluation of progress of counter-IED efforts in Pakistan. State committed to improve assessment of its programs by looking for ways to broaden the scope of existing metrics in order to better reflect and evaluate interagency participation in counter-IED efforts. In its comments, DHS noted that it is committed to working with interagency partners to improve abilities for tracking counter-IED efforts in Pakistan. DOD provided technical comments that were incorporated, as appropriate. DOJ responded that it did not have any comments on the draft report.

As agreed with your office, unless you publicly announce the contents of this report earlier, we plan no further distribution until 30 days from the report date. At that time, we will send copies to appropriate congressional committees, the Secretaries of State, Homeland Security, and Defense, as well as the Attorney General of the United States. In addition, the report will be available at no charge on the GAO website at http://www.gao.gov.

If you or your staff have any questions about this report, please contact me at (202) 512-7331 or johnsoncm@gao.gov. Contact points for our Offices of Congressional Relations and Public Affairs may be found on the last page of this report. GAO staff who made key contributions to this report are listed in appendix IV.

Sincerely yours,

Charles Michael Johnson, Jr., Director
International Affairs and Trade

# Appendix I: Scope and Methodology

To describe the status of U.S. efforts to assist Pakistan in countering improvised explosive devices (IEDs), we reviewed agency documentation of relevant activities since 2010. In addition, we reviewed the Pakistan National Counter-IED Strategy and draft National Implementation Plan to gain knowledge of the areas that Pakistan has focused on in seeking assistance from the international community. We inventoried and described the efforts of U.S. agencies to assist Pakistan in countering IEDs and preventing the smuggling of calcium ammonium nitrate (CAN) and other IED precursors from Pakistan to Afghanistan. We analyzed funding and program information on specific projects and activities and followed up with interviews with knowledgeable U.S. officials and international partners to obtain their views on efforts to assist Pakistan to counter IEDs and prevent the smuggling of CAN and other precursors. We interviewed officials from the Departments of (State), Homeland Security (DHS), and Justice (DOJ), in Washington, D.C., and the Department of Defense (DOD) in Arlington, Virginia, and Tampa, Florida, as well as representatives of all these agencies at the U.S. Embassy in Pakistan. Specifically, in Pakistan we interviewed representatives from State's Economic, Political, Narcotics Affairs, and Public Affairs sections; DHS's Homeland Security Investigations office; DOJ's, Drug Enforcement Administration and Legal Attaché; and DOD's Office of Defense Representative, Pakistan, and Strategic Interagency Assistance Team. The international partners we interviewed included representatives from the United Nations Office on Drugs and Crime, the British High Commission, and the International Security Assistance Force International Coordination Element–Pakistan. We also interviewed Pakistani customs officials from the Directorate General of the Intelligence and Investigations and the Federal Board of Revenue to obtain their perspective on counter-IED efforts and challenges. During our January 2012 trip to Pakistan to learn more about the use of CAN and other fertilizers, we met with U.S. Department of Agriculture Animal and Plant Health Inspection Service officials as well as with representatives of the Pakistan National Fertilizer Development Center, but we were unable to meet with other Pakistani officials or representatives of the Pakistani company that manufactures CAN fertilizer. To learn more about Afghanistan and Pakistan border issues, we met with representatives from the Pakistan Trade Project, a U.S. Agency for International Development partner who provided video footage of the Chaman and Torkham border crossings between Pakistan and Afghanistan.

To review State's tracking of U.S. assisted efforts in Pakistan to counter IEDs, we reviewed State's fiscal year 2013 Mission Strategic and Resource Plan for the U.S. Mission in Pakistan. Specifically, we reviewed goals, performance indicators, and targets for counterterrorism and counterinsurgency; regional security, stability, and nonproliferation; law enforcement reform and rule of law; and public diplomacy and strategic communications to identify the extent to which they covered counter-IED efforts. We also followed up with a State official at the U.S, Embassy in Pakistan with regard to how targets under the new counter-IED performance indicator in the MSRP track progress of counter-IED efforts. The information on foreign law in this report is not the product of GAO's original analysis, but is derived from interviews and secondary sources.

We conducted this performance audit from October 2011 to May 2012 in accordance with generally accepted government auditing standards. Those standards require that we plan and perform the audit to obtain sufficient, appropriate evidence to provide a reasonable basis for our findings and conclusions based on our audit objectives. We believe that the evidence obtained provides a reasonable basis for our findings and conclusions based on our audit objectives.

# Appendix II: Comments from the Department of State

United States Department of State

*Chief Financial Officer*

*Washington, D.C. 20520*

May 8, 2012

Mr. Loren Yager
Managing Director
International Affairs and Trade
Government Accountability Office
441 G Street, N.W.
Washington, D.C. 20548-0001

Dear Mr. Yager:

We appreciate the opportunity to review your draft report, "COMBATING TERRORISM: State Should Enhance Its Performance measures for Assessing Efforts in Pakistan to Counter Improvised Explosive Devices," GAO Job Code 320872.

The enclosed Department of State comments are provided for incorporation with this letter as an appendix to the final report.

If you have any questions concerning this response, please contact Amy Flohr, Pakistan Desk Officer, Bureau of South and Central Asian Affairs at (202) 647-5882.

Sincerely,

James L. Millette

cc:   GAO – Charles M. Johnson
      SCA– Robert O. Blake, Jr.
      State/OIG – Evelyn Klemstine

**Department of State Comments on GAO Draft Report**

**COMBATING TERRORISM: State Should Enhance Its Performance
Measures for Assessing Efforts in Pakistan to Counter
Improvised Explosive Devices
(GAO-12-614, GAO Code 320872)**

Thank you for the opportunity to comment on your draft report entitled,
*"Combating Terrorism: State Should Enhance Its Performance Measures for
Assessing Efforts in Pakistan to Counter Improvised Explosive Devices.*

The Department of State acknowledges the GAO's recommendation for enhanced
performance measures of U.S. assisted efforts to counter the production and
proliferation of improvised explosive devices (IEDs) in Pakistan. We concur with
GAO's assessment that comprehensive metrics would better enable us to evaluate
progress on this important effort. As such, State will seek to improve assessment of
its programs and will look for ways to broaden the scope of existing metrics in
order to better reflect and evaluate the robust interagency participation in this effort.

# Appendix III: Comments from the Department of Homeland Security

U.S. Department of Homeland Security
Washington, DC 20528

May 4, 2012

Charles Michael Johnson, Jr.
Director, International Affairs and Trade
U.S. Government Accountability Office
441 G Street, NW
Washington, DC 20548

Re: Draft Report GAO-12-614, "COMBATING TERRORISM: State Should Enhance Its
Performance Measures for Assessing Efforts in Pakistan to Counter Improvised Explosive
Devices"

Dear Mr. Johnson:

Thank you for the opportunity to review and comment on this draft report. The U.S. Department
of Homeland Security (DHS) appreciates the U.S. Government Accountability Office's (GAO)
work in planning and conducting its review and issuing this report.

The Department is pleased to note GAO's recognition of DHS's support in providing counter-
improvised explosive device (IED) assistance to Pakistan, including counter-IED and border
protection training and equipment. For example, Program Global Shield, an international effort
to eliminate the smuggling of chemicals used by terrorists and insurgents, was conceptualized by
U.S. Immigration and Customs Enforcement personnel in 2010. Global Shield marked the first
time that police and customs officials from around the world had joined forces to keep bomb-
making precursor chemicals out of the hands of terrorist and criminal organizations. Global
Shield partners have seized more than 33 metric tons of material used to produce IEDs and made
19 arrests in various countries across the globe. These chemicals could have been used to
manufacture thousands of IEDs.

Although the report does not contain any recommendations specifically directed to DHS, the
Department remains committed to continuing its work with interagency partners such as the U.S.
Department of State and others. This includes work related to improving abilities for tracking
progress of efforts in Pakistan to counter IEDs, as appropriate.

Again, thank you for the opportunity to review and comment on this draft report. We look
forward to working with you on future Homeland Security issues.

Sincerely,

Jim H. Crumpacker
Director
Departmental GAO-OIG Liaison Office

# Appendix IV: GAO Contact and Staff Acknowledgments

| | |
|---|---|
| **GAO Contact** | Charles Michael Johnson, Jr., (202) 512-7331 or johnsoncm@gao.gov |
| **Staff Acknowledgments** | In addition to the individual named above, Jason Bair, Assistant Director; David Dayton, Eddie Uyekawa; and Tom Zingale made key contributions to this report. Alissa Czyz, David Dornisch, Mark Dowling, Carol E. Finkler, Brandon Hunt, Theresa Perkins, Cary Russell, Kira Self, and Yong Song provided additional support. |

www.ingramcontent.com/pod-product-compliance
Lightning Source LLC
Chambersburg PA
CBHW080943290526

45795CB00007BA/2878